Rick Pieros Photography

1878-2012

Jackson Hole

Historical Photographs

Past to Present™

About the Author & Photographer

Rick Pieros has been traveling the rural and wild areas of the western United States since his youth. Drawn to the remnants of the American West's rich and colorful past, Rick switched from a path solely pursuing nature photography to follow his passion for documenting the quickly vanishing artifacts of the western experience. In addition to his Jackson Hole photographic work, Rick's complementary interest is in the abstract details of weathered detritus: miner's shacks, abandoned automobiles, mining equipment, and other items abandoned to be patinaed by the elements.

Rick owned and operated Wild Spirits Nature Photography studio on historic Main Street in Park City, Utah until 2007. He currently lives at the base of the Wasatch Mountains with his wife Heidi and two daughters, Hailey and Ivy. To view Rick's portfolio of Jackson Hole and Grand Teton National Park images, or to order limited edition photographs, please visit: www.RickPieros.com

Additional information on *Jackson Hole 1878 to 2012: Historical Photographs Past to Present* can be found by visiting www.jacksonholepasttopresent.com.

Publisher Information:
Rick Pieros
Rick Pieros Photography
P.O. Box 982181
Park City, Utah 84098

ISBN 978-0-578-09761-9

Front Cover Photograph:
Moulton Barn, Mormon Row,
Grand Teton National Park, 2010.

Back Cover Photographs:
Jackson 1907, Jackson, 2011.

Printed in China by Global GSD.

Author-Photographer, Great Salt Lake, Utah, 2010.

Whitebark Pine, Grand Teton National Park, 2011.

Acknowledgements

The journey of writing, photographing, and publishing *Jackson Hole 1878 to 2012: Historical Photographs Past to Present* has been an extraordinary experience. There were many helping hands along the way. I would like to personally thank Mindy Barnett, Jean Hansen, and Lokey Lytjen of the Jackson Hole Historical Society & Museum for their invaluable knowledge and assistance. I would also like to thank Alice Hart of Grand Teton National Park for her helpful research. All of the historic photographs in *Jackson Hole 1878 to 2012: Historical Photographs Past to Present* are used by permission of the Jackson Hole Historical Society & Museum, Grand Teton National Park, Signal Mountain Lodge, National Archives & Records Administration, and the American Heritage Center. All individual photography credits can be found at the end of the book.

Anna Katherine Curfman deserves special thanks for her expertise and assistance in shepherding *Jackson Hole 1878 to 2012: Historical Photographs Past to Present* through the publishing process. I would also like to thank Corbet Curfman of Riverbed Design for his brilliant, yet simple book design. Most importantly, I would like to thank my wife Heidi and daughters Hailey and Ivy. This book would have been impossible without their support and encouragement. Finally, I would like to express gratitude to all my friends and family that I have shared time and fond memories with in Jackson and Grand Teton National Park.

T.A. Moulton barn, Mormon Row, Grand Teton National Park, 2006.

Jackson Rodeo Grounds, circa early 1900's.

Contents

Discovery of Jackson Hole 6
- 1872 Hayden Expedition 6
- Jackson Lake & William Henry Jackson 7

Faith in a Better Life: Early Settlers & Pioneers 8
- Karnes Cabin 8
- Cunningham Cabin 9
- Menor's Ferry 10
- Manges Cabin 12
- Norman Smith Homestead 13
- Sargent Homestead 14
- Mormon Row 16
- Miller House 18
- National Elk Refuge 19
- Wilson 20
- Kelly 21

The Founding of Jackson 22
- The Founding of Jackson 22
- Teton Pass 23
- Jackson Overlook 24
- Clubhouse & Jackson Mercantile Co. 26
- Deloney's General Merchandise 28
- Hotel Jackson 29
- St. John's Episcopal Church 30
- The Coe Cabin 32
- Crabtree Hotel 33
- Jackson State Bank 34
- American Legion Hall 35
- Spicer Garage 36
- Jackson Hole Playhouse 37
- Simpson Hardware 38
- Miller House 39
- Van Vleck House 40

1920 Jackson Town Council 41
Jackson Drug Company 42
Mercill's General Merchandise 44
Silver Spur Café 45
Cowboy Bar 46
Teton Theater 48
Jackson Town Square 50
Jackson-Wilson High School 51
The Wort Hotel 52
The Motel Era 54
Kudar Motel 55

Frontier Days: 100 Years of the Jackson Hole Rodeo 56
Mickey Hicks 56
Frontier Days 57

Dude Ranching in Jackson Hole 58
Early Days of Dude Ranching 58
The Jackson Hole Gang 59
White Grass Ranch 60
The Western Center for Historic Preservation 61
Bar BC Ranch 62
Triangle X Ranch 64
Elbo Ranch 66
Danny Ranch 68
Jenny Lake Lodge 69
4 Lazy F Ranch 70

Grand Teton National Park 72
Grand Teton National Park 72
Jenny Lake Junction 73
Moran & Jackson Lake Dam 74
Harrison Crandall Studio 75
The Chapel of the Transfiguration 76
Jenny Lake 78
Moose — Dornans 80
Signal Mountain Lodge 81
Jackson Lake Lodge 82

Skiing in Jackson Hole: A Brief History 84
Snow King Resort 84
Jackson Hole Mountain Resort 85

Cinema in Jackson Hole 86

Afterword: The Sundance Inn 87

Photography Credits & Notes 88

The Discovery of Jackson Hole

The discovery of Jackson Hole has its roots in the expansion of the fur trade into the Rocky Mountain region. The first travelers to Jackson Hole included the mountain man John Colter, as well as the members of John Jacob Astor's American Fur Company, who passed through in the early 1800's. Jackson Hole primarily remained the domain of Native Americans until the 1830's, when Jackson Hole became a major crossroads for trapper trails and mountain men. The heyday of the fur trade lasted until around 1840, when trends in fashion caused beaver pelt prices to crash, bringing about the end of an era. It was not until United States Government Surveys of the 1860's and the 1870's did Jackson Hole again see significant exploration. The most important of the surveys was the Hayden Expedition of 1872. The Hayden Expedition collected thousands of plant and animal specimens, studied the geology the area, and mapped the Teton Range. The Hayden Survey also gave many place names to land features in Jackson Hole including Mount Moran, Phelps Lake, Leigh Lake, and Mount Leidy among others.

Hayden Expedition, circa 1872.

Mount Moran and Jackson Lake, circa 1878.

Mount Moran and Jackson Lake, 2011.

William Henry Jackson, 1872.

Jackson Lake & William Henry Jackson

As a member of the Hayden Expedition of 1878, William Henry Jackson was able to capture the first known photographs from Jackson Hole. Jackson was a veteran of previous Hayden Expeditions to Yellowstone and the Rocky Mountains, and his photographs helped convince the United States Congress to create Yellowstone National Park in 1872. Jackson later went on to become an accomplished painter, as well as a publisher. A veteran of the Civil War, William Henry Jackson is buried in Arlington National Cemetery. Mount Jackson in the Gallatin Range of Yellowstone National Park is named in his honor.

Trapper "Beaver Dick" Leigh, date unknown.

Faith in a Better Life: Early Settlers & Pioneers

Originally the domain of Native Americans, trappers, and mountain men, Jackson Hole was settled in the 1880's by a hardy collection of pioneers, hunters, ranchers, and farmers. The first permanent settlers of Jackson Hole were a diverse collection of individuals looking to scratch out a living from the rugged landscape in the shadow of the Teton Range. The first individuals to homestead in Jackson Hole were John Holland, John Karnes and his wife Millie Sorelle in 1884. Others followed, leaving behind homes in search of a better life. Named in 1894, the early town of Jackson was situated in a location central to many of the small family ranches in the area. By 1900, the population of the Jackson Hole valley had grown from a few families and bachelors to over 600 individuals. Today, Jackson and the surrounding valley of Jackson Hole is home to nearly 10,000 souls who still possess the pioneering spirit of the original homesteaders.

Karnes Cabin, 2011.

Cunningham Cabin, 2011.

Cunningham Cabin, 1996.

Cunningham Cabin

One of the first settlers to arrive in Jackson Hole was J. Pierce Cunningham in 1885. The twenty-year-old Pierce spent his first couple of years in Jackson Hole trapping. Pierce later homesteaded south of Spread Creek with his wife Margaret. Established as the Bar Flying U Ranch, the ranch eventually grew to include a ranch house, barn, tack shed, and outbuildings, as well as the original "dog-trot" style homestead cabin still standing today. After many years of hardships associated with ranching in such an unforgiving climate, the Cunninghams sold their Bar Flying U Ranch to the Snake River Land Company in 1928.

Bill Menor, date unknown.

Menor's Ferry

Bill Menor homesteaded along the west bank of the Snake River near present-day Moose, Wyoming in 1894. Menor constructed a ferry which became the major river crossing for early settlers of Jackson Hole. Menor's homestead consisted of a five-room cabin, storage shed, blacksmith shop, barn, and 149 fenced acres. During the 1890's Menor was the only settler on the west side of the Snake River. In 1918, Bill Menor sold his ferry and homestead to Maude Noble, who hoped to earn a living from the growing tourist traffic in the valley. Maude also ran what was called the Ferry Ranch Store. Unfortunately for Noble, a steel truss bridge was constructed south of the ferry in 1927, rendering it obsolete. Maude Noble sold her property to John D. Rockefeller Jr.'s Snake River Land Company in 1929. In 1949, Rockefeller donated a restored Menor's Ferry and homestead to the National Park Service. The Bill Menor homestead was listed on the National Register of Historic Places in 1969. Grand Teton National Park operates the historic Menor's Ferry each summer for visitors to experience a small part of pioneer life in Jackson Hole.

Menor's Ferry, circa 1899.

Menor's Ferry, date unknown.

Above: Bill Menor's cabin, 2011. Below: Menor's Ferry, 2011.

Remnant, original ferryboat pontoon, 2011.

Manges Cabin & Pasture, 2012.

Manges Cabin

James Manges arrived in Jackson Hole in 1910 and built a cabin in 1911 near Taggart Creek. Manges became the second settler on the west side of the Snake River after Bill Menor. The Manges Cabin was reported to be the first two-story structure in the northern part of the Jackson Hole valley. The log and frame structure featured wide eaves to keep the winter snow away from the walls, and was heated in the winter by a single stove. Later, the Manges Cabin became part of a larger ranch with guest cabins, resembling more of a dude ranch than a working cattle ranch. James Manges sold his ranch in 1926 to Chester Goss who renamed the property the Elbo Ranch. The Manges Cabin was listed on the National Register of Historic Places in 1998.

Above: Manges Cabin, circa 1930's. Below: Manges Cabin, 2010.

Above: Norman Smith Homestead, circa 1912. Below: Blacktail Butte, 2011.

Norman Smith Homestead

Norman Smith settled along with his family on the northwest side of Blacktail Butte in 1908. The Smith family arrived in Jackson Hole by happen stance. Bound for Colorado, the Smith's had a series of misfortunes while traveling through Jackson Hole. After crossing the Snake River at Menor's ferry, the family camped near Blacktail Butte and decided staying was their best option. Norman Smith built a log house in 1908–1909 and over the next several years cleared over 100 acres for cultivation. By 1919, Norman Smith had "proved-up" his land claim under the Homestead Act of 1862, and gained title to his property free and clear with the payment of a $15 fee. The Smith family had one of the more productive farms in the area and made a decent living for many years. In 1931, an elderly Norman Smith sold his property to the Snake River Land Company. Today, the Norman Smith Homestead has returned to a mostly natural state.

Edith Drake Sargent, circa 1910.

Sargent Homestead

John Dudley Sargent arrived in Jackson Hole in 1890 and settled on the eastern shore of Jackson Lake with his wife Adelaide and five children. At the time, the Sargent homestead represented the northernmost homestead in the Jackson Hole valley. By 1891, Sargent had completed a ten-room log house with a sod roof, which he called Marymere, to house his family. Other structures at the homestead included a barn and corrals, woodshed, chicken house, and boathouse. Controversy surrounded John Dudley Sargent much of his life in Jackson Hole. The death of his business partner, Robert Ray Hamilton in 1890, and wife Adelaide later in 1897, both happened under unusual circumstances. Additionally, Sargent's second wife Edith Drake Sargent was rumored to be mentally ill and was frequently seen playing her violin in the nude while perched in a curved spruce tree overlooking Jackson Lake. Sargent himself was reported to suffer from depression, and eventually took his own life in the summer of 1913. Today, the Sargent homestead and related buildings have vanished and been reclaimed by native lodgepole pine forest, which have grown to obstruct the view that the Sargent homestead once enjoyed.

View south toward Sargent Bay, Jackson Lake, 2011.

Left: John Moulton homestead, circa 1940's. Above: John Moulton barn, 2010.

Kestrel atop the "Pink House", 1999.

Mormon Row

In the late 1800's, leaders of The Church of Jesus Christ of Latter-day Saints, or Mormons, sent parties from the Salt Lake Valley to establish new communities to support their burgeoning population. Mormon homesteaders who settled east of Blacktail Butte, closely assembled their farms to share labor and community, which mirrored their collective efforts in the Salt Lake Valley. These settlers first arrived in the 1890's from Idaho, establishing a community originally named Grovont by the U.S. Post Office. Homesteaders established 27 homesteads in the Grovont area because of relatively fertile soil, shelter from winds by Blacktail Butte and access to the Gros Ventre River. Despite the harsh conditions found in the shadow of the Teton Range, Mormon settlers grew crops by using irrigation methods first tested with the settlement of the Salt Lake Valley. These hardy settlers dug ditches by hand and with teams of horses, built a complex network of levees and dikes to funnel water from central ditches to their fields between 1896 and 1937. The area is known today as "Mormon Row" and is a favorite spot for photographers from around the world to frame a bucolic scene of John Moulton's two-story gambrel barn as a foreground for the magnificent Teton Range. The Mormon Row Historic District was added to the National Register of Historic Places in 1997.

Robert and Grace Miller, Miller House, circa 1905.

Miller House, National Elk Refuge, 2011.

Miller House

Robert Miller ventured to Jackson Hole in 1885, and staked a homestead claim on what is now the National Elk Refuge. Being only the third homestead claim in the valley, Miller was able to select an advantageous location near a productive spring. Robert Miller returned back east in 1893 to marry Grace Green. In 1895, the newlywed couple returned to Jackson Hole and began construction on what is now known as the Miller House. Considered luxurious in an era of sod-roofed cabins, the Miller House was an epicenter of social activity during the late 1800's and early 1900's as settlers traveled into the valley from various regions. The Millers sold their ranch to the Federal Government in 1914 to augment the newly created National Elk Refuge.

Miller House, National Elk Refuge, 2011.

Above: Miller House, 2012. Below: Elk herd, Miller House, National Elk Refuge, circa 1930's.

National Elk Refuge

The National Elk Refuge was established in 1912 in response to local outcry concerning the declining elk herds in the Jackson Hole area. Through private land purchases, land donations from The Izaak Walton League of America, and Presidential Executive Orders, the National Elk Refuge was expanded to nearly 25,000 acres by 1936. Today, the National Elk Refuge represents the last remaining elk winter range for the Jackson Hole Elk Herd, which winter on a mere one-quarter of their historic winter range.

Neighboring Communities - Wilson

Wilson was pioneered in 1889 by the family of Elijah Nicholas Wilson, and was later named in his honor. Situated at the eastern base of Teton Pass, Wilson benefited early on from its location along the Teton Pass road. By 1898, Wilson boasted a hotel, saloon, general store, and a post office.

Wilson Post Office, circa early 1900's.

Wilson Post Office, 2011.

Hungry Jack's, Wilson, 2011.

Above: Gros Ventre slide, 2011. Below: Kelly, 2011.

Former Episcopal Church, circa late 1920's.

Kelly

Kelly was settled in the late 1890's by the William Kelly family. By 1909, the town boasted a timber bridge spanning the Gros Ventre River, as well as a school. Later in 1914, the town had grown to include a general store, hotel, blacksmith shop, and a post office. The town enjoyed prosperity during the early 1920's, and even rivaled Jackson for the county seat with the creation of Teton County in 1921. In June of 1925, an estimated fifty million cubic yards of rock slid off the north face of Sheep Mountain and into the Gros Ventre River Canyon below. The slide eventually stabilized and formed Slide Lake above the Town of Kelly. Two years later, fueled by heavy rain and snowmelt, the Gros Ventre spilled over the dam, which soon failed. On May 18, 1927, the town was destroyed, save the school and the church, which was soon converted into a post office and general store.

Above: Teton Pass, circa 1950's. Below: Teton Pass, 2011.

The Founding of Jackson

Originally the domain of Native Americans, trappers, and mountain men, Jackson Hole was settled in the 1880's by a hardy collection of pioneers, hunters, ranchers, and farmers. The first permanent settlers of Jackson Hole were a diverse collection of individuals looking to scratch out a living from the rugged landscape in the shadow of the Teton Range. Named in 1894, the early town of Jackson was situated in a location central to many of the small family ranches in the area. By 1900, the population of the Jackson Hole valley had grown from a few families and bachelors to over 600 individuals. Today, Jackson and the surrounding valley of Jackson Hole is home to nearly 10,000 souls who still possess the pioneering spirit of the original homesteaders.

Above: Teton Pass, circa early 1900's. Below: Wyoming State Highway 22, Teton Pass, 2011.

Teton Pass

Once one of the main routes into Jackson Hole for Native Americans and trappers, Teton Pass became the main route for supplies and mail into Jackson Hole for settlers and pioneers. Supplies arrived and departed via railroad lines in Idaho. Due to the importance of Teton Pass to the economic well being of Jackson Hole, "The Pass" as it was known, came to occupy a prominent place in everyday life and conversation. Today, Teton Pass still plays a central role to the Jackson Hole economy. Many individuals who work in Jackson make the daily commute from the towns of Victor and Driggs, Idaho on the west side of "The Pass".

Town of Jackson, circa 1907.

Jackson Overlook, 1907

The Town of Jackson from the east side of East Gros Ventre Butte as it looked in 1907. The photograph captured by William Trester is a glimpse of a hardscrabble community on the edge of the frontier. Visible structures along the sagebrush flat include the Clubhouse, Deloney's General Merchandise, and the Hotel Jackson.

Town of Jackson, 2011.

Jackson Overlook, 2011

The Town of Jackson as it looked in the summer of 2011. The Clubhouse, just left of center is still visible and occupies a prominent spot on the east side of the Jackson Town Square. Other prominent changes to the skyline of Jackson include the Wort Hotel, the Jackson Hole Center for the Arts, and the Snow King Resort & Convention Center.

Clubhouse Building, Jackson Mercantile Co., circa early 1900's.

Clubhouse Building & Jackson Mercantile Co.

The Clubhouse Building was constructed in 1897 by the Jackson Hole Gun Club and became one of the social centers of Jackson. The two-story rectangular building served as the town's first courthouse, as well as a school, gymnasium, gentleman's smoking room, and dance hall. Later, the Clubhouse became one of Jackson's first commercial buildings when the Jackson Mercantile Co. opened in 1906. Today, the Clubhouse Building still stands on the east side of the Jackson Town Square and houses several local businesses.

Clubhouse Building, 2012.

Deloney's General Merchandise, circa 1916.

Jackson Hole Historical Society Museum, 2011.

Deloney's General Merchandise

Charles "Pap" Deloney opened the first general store in Jackson Hole in 1906. The store offered a generous variety of merchandise including hardware, groceries, farm equipment, dry goods, and groceries. The building was constructed of locally produced brick that was used on several buildings constructed in the early 1900's including the first Jackson State Bank. The brick proved to be unsuited to Jackson Hole's harsh climate and eroded quickly. The Deloney's General Merchandise building was able to withstand the elements by the addition of a chicken wire and cement façade. The building formerly housed the Jackson Hole Historical Society Museum and is the last brick building remaining in Jackson from the turn of the century. The new museum is located at 225 N Cache Street in downtown Jackson.

Legacy Gallery, 2011. Below: Hotel Jackson, circa 1907. (Left to Right) Robert Miller, Pierce Cunningham, Long Tom Imeson, and Butch Robinson.

Hotel Jackson

The Hotel Jackson was originally built by Mary Anderson and was located near Antelope Gap. The hotel was subsequently moved to the Town of Jackson in 1901. Peter Nelson expanded the hotel in 1905, after he acquired it from Mrs. Anderson, by adding a two-story brick wing to the rear of the original structure. Nelson later sold the Hotel Jackson to Pierce Cunningham, who was among the first settlers to Jackson Hole and became one of its most prominent early citizens.

St. John's Episcopal Church, 2011.

Above: St. John's Episcopal Church, Rest House, and Hospital, circa 1918. Below: St. John's Rest House, 2011.

St. John's Episcopal Church

The St. John's Episcopal Church Rest House was built in 1911 to provide for social services in the growing Jackson Hole community. The Rest House provided shelter for individuals passing through the area that needed a place to overnight and could not afford a hotel. The facility included a library, vicar's quarters, and a billiards table. The Rest House was used as a meeting hall, school classroom, and for church services until 1916, when the church was built. The hospital was also constructed in 1916 and served the Jackson Hole community until 1960, when a new, larger hospital was constructed near the National Elk Refuge. The St. John's Church and Rest House are both on the National Register of Historic Places.

Above: Coe Cabin, circa 1920's. Below: Sweetwater Restaurant, 2011.

Coe Cabin

The Coe Cabin was originally built by Clarence and Martha Dow in 1915. Long-time Jackson residents Ed and Emily Coe, who operated a nearby blacksmith shop, lived in the cabin for many years and constructed the northern additions to the original log cabin. The Coe Cabin became the Sweetwater Restaurant in 1976, and today features the cuisine of owner/executive chef Trey Davis.

Above: Crabtree Hotel, circa 1920's. Below: Crabtree Corner, 2012.

Crabtree Hotel

The Crabtree Hotel was built in 1907 as an infirmary. Doc Palmer, an early Jackson physician, sold the building in 1909 to Maud and Claude Reed. The Reeds, who hailed from Arkansas, operated the Reed Hotel as a hotel and boarding house. In 1917, Reed employees Rose and Henry Crabtree took over the hotel after "Ma" Reed boarded a stagecoach for a two-week trip, and didn't return for seven years. In 1992, the Crabtree Hotel was demolished due to its dilapidated state. Today, a replica building known as Crabtree Corner occupies the same spot.

Jackson State Bank, circa 1925.
(Left to Right) Jim Francis, Robert Miller, R.P. Stevens, and Charlie Fox.

Original Jackson State Bank, circa early 1900's. Cashier Harry Wagner & dog Muggins.

Jackson State Bank

Recognizing a need for a banking institution in the valley, Roger Miller organized the Jackson State Bank in 1914. The bank was originally located in a brick building on the west side of the Town Square. Built of the same soft brick as "Pap" Deloney's General Store, the bank did not last long in Jackson Hole's harsh climate. The Jackson State Bank was rebuilt in a different location on Broadway Avenue next to "Ma" Reed's hotel. Today, both Jackson State Bank buildings have faded into memory. Jackson State Bank served the Jackson Hole community for many years until the institution was sold to Wells Fargo Bank in 2008.

Crabtree Corner, 2011.

Above: American Legion Hall, circa 1930's. Below: American Legion Hall, 2011.

American Legion Hall

American Legion Post Number 43 was founded in 1920. The Jackson Hole American Legion Hall was built in 1929 after nine years of fund raising. The cope-cornered log structure has served a wide range of social uses and community activities in Jackson Hole over the years. The American Legion Hall was restored in 2001 and placed on the U.S. National Register of Historic Places in 2002.

Spicer Garage, circa 1920's.

Spicer Garage

The Spicer Garage was built by "Pap" Deloney in 1916. The garage was leased by Walt Spicer and became Jackson's first Ford dealership. The building has a long and storied history including stints as a blacksmith shop, freight office, bowling alley, and a bus depot.

Jackson Hole Playhouse, 2011.

Saddlerock Family Saloon interior, 2011.

Jackson Hole Playhouse

In 1958, the Spicer Garage was turned into the Pink Garter Theater. When the Pink Garter moved to Broadway Avenue, the Spicer Garage became the Jackson Hole Playhouse & Saddle Rock Family Saloon. The Jackson Hole Playhouse features such Broadway musical favorites as *Big River, Oklahoma, Calamity Jane, The Sound of Music, The Unsinkable Molly Brown,* and *Seven Brides for Seven Brothers* and is a favorite among tourists and locals.

Simpson Hardware

Simpson Hardware was located on the south side of the Town Square and boasted the town's first gas pump in 1922. The store offered a wide variety of merchandise and hardware to Jackson Hole residents. The original building, although significantly modified, still stands on the south side of the Town Square.

Left: Jackson Hole Hardware Building, 2011. Above: Simpson Hardware, circa 1920's. (Left to Right) Chester Simpson and Don Williams.

Miller House, 2011.

Miller House

Robert and Grace Miller built this home in Jackson in 1921 after they sold their original homestead to help foster the creation of the National Elk Refuge. Robert and Grace were both influential citizens in the early history and development of Jackson Hole. In the early 1900's, Grace and Maggie Simpson planned and platted the original Jackson town site. Grace was also elected Jackson's first female Mayor in 1920, leading one of the first all-woman town governments in the United States. The Miller House has been well preserved and is currently home to the offices of Wyoming Title & Escrow.

Miller House, circa 1930's.

Van Vleck House, circa 1930's.

Van Vleck House

Roy Van Vleck came to Jackson in 1906 with his brother Frank and opened the Jackson Mercantile Company. Later, Roy Van Vleck built this home in 1910 for his bride-to-be Genevieve. Both Roy and Genevieve became prominent citizens in Jackson. Roy planted the large cottonwood trees that still line Broadway, while Genevieve was elected part of the first all-woman town council in 1920. After housing Jed's House of Sourdough restaurant for many years, the Van Vleck House is now home to Café Genevieve, which prides itself on warm western hospitality and exceptional cuisine prepared by Executive Chef/Partner Joshua Governale. Fred Peightal is the managing partner of Café Genevieve and can be found most days personally welcoming guests to the restaurant.

Café Genevieve, 2011.

Jackson Mayor & Town Council, circa 1920's. (Left to Right) Mae Deloney, Rose Crabtree, Mayor Grace Miller, Faustina Haight, Genevieve Van Vleck.

Jackson Mayor & Town Council, 2012.
(Left to Right) Greg Miles, Mayor Mark Barron, Melissa Turley, Bob Lenz, and Mark Obringer (not pictured).

1920 Jackson Town Council

In 1920, the Town of Jackson elected one of the first all-women civic governments in the United States. The election was fitting for Jackson, considering that Wyoming was the first state to grant women the right to vote in 1869. Additionally, the Wyoming State Motto is "Equal Rights".

Jackson Drug Company, circa 1940's.

Jackson Drug Company

Bruce Porter built the Jackson Drug Company building in 1937. The structure was constructed from volcanic stone quarried from a volcanic deposit on the west side of Teton Pass, near Victor, Idaho. The Jackson Drug Company was originally located in the Clubhouse Building, and occupied that space from 1912 to 1937. Porter transported the original marble bar area and mosaic tiles from the original Clubhouse drugstore to his new building. Jackson Drug Company was known for their soda fountain. Among the usual fare, the soda fountain featured homemade ice cream, which was made in the cellar of the building. Jackson Drug Company closed in 2001.

Above: Davies–Reid, 2012. Below: interior, Davies–Reid, 2011. Right: detail, Original Jackson Drug Bar, 2011.

In 2001, Davies–Reid opened in the former Jackson Drug Company Building. The brainchild of Sharon Davies and Terry Reid, Davies–Reid is a specialty retailer that offers a wide variety of unique rugs, textiles, home décor, and intricate architectural elements from around the world. As an homage to the past, the Davies–Reid building still features the original Jackson Drug Company bar & soda fountain.

Mercill's General Merchandise, circa 1950's.

Mercill's General Merchandise

Billy Mercill opened his store in 1913, and originally called his establishment "Mercill's Big Country Store". Mercill's was known to offer everything from boots to vegetables. Today, the former Mercill's building is home to Wyoming Outfitters, a specialty retailer of outdoor clothing, jewelry, home décor, and accessories. The building still retains original elements, including the hardwood floors and tin ceiling tiles.

Wyoming Outfitters, 2011.

Silver Spur Café, circa 1965.

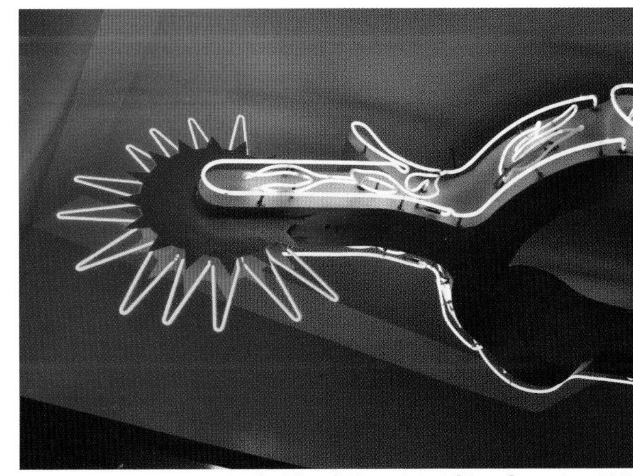

Interior, the Cadillac Grille, original Silver Spur sign, 2011.

The Cadillac Grille, 2011.

Silver Spur Café

The Silver Spur Café opened in the building formerly occupied by Moore's Café on the west side of the Town Square. Considered "upscale" during the 1950's and 1960's, the Silver Spur was a favorite stop for locals and tourists. Today, the former Moore's Café and Silver Spur Café building is the Cadillac Grille, which was established by Ken Rominger and Suzanne Marino in 1983.

Cowboy Bar, circa 1941.

Cowboy Bar

The Cowboy Bar was originally known as Joe Ruby's Café and Beer Garden, and was built on the site of the original Jackson State Bank in the 1930's. According to local legend, Joe Ruby was asked to leave town after a card-game argument and shooting at the café. A local rancher named Ben Goe purchased the bar and renamed it the Cowboy Bar. Goe remodeled the establishment adding silver dollars to the bar top, burled pine woodwork, and western murals. While gambling in Wyoming has been illegal since 1901, gambling in remote Teton County remained common throughout the 1930's and 1940's. The Cowboy Bar was no exception, and featured its share of card tables, roulette wheels, and slot machines. To the right of the Cowboy Bar is Moore's Café, which was owned by Jack and Helen Moore.

Million Dollar Cowboy Bar, 2011.

Million Dollar Cowboy Bar

Preston Parkinson purchased the Cowboy Bar from Ben Goe around 1945. Parkinson added the classic neon cowboy sign in 1953 that is considered by many visitors to be synonymous with the Town of Jackson. Parkinson was also responsible for the addition of the appellation "Million Dollar" to the Cowboy Bar establishment after renovations were required as a result of a gas explosion in the basement. Today, the Million Dollar Cowboy Bar has the distinction of being the oldest existing business on the Town Square, and still retains the western character that has made it a favorite with locals and tourists alike. Since 1988, the Million Dollar Cowboy Bar has been owned by Art & Carol Andersen and Hagan Dudley & the late Roger Dudley, who are committed to retaining the historic character of the bar as a vital part of Wyoming history.

Interior, Million Dollar Cowboy Bar, 2011.

Cowboy Bar sign, 2003.

Teton Theater sign, 2007.

Teton Theater

The Teton Theater was constructed in 1941 by Bruce Porter as both a cinema and stage production theater. The theater is constructed from the same volcanic stone quarried from a volcanic deposit on the west side of Teton Pass as the original Jackson Drug Company building situated to the south. Originally the theater did not have a concession stand. Thus, patrons would purchase their refreshments prior to the movie next door at Jackson Drug. The Teton Theater is still in business today, offering patrons a vintage cinema experience in an original single-screen theater.

Teton Theater, circa 1940's.

Teton Theater, 2011.

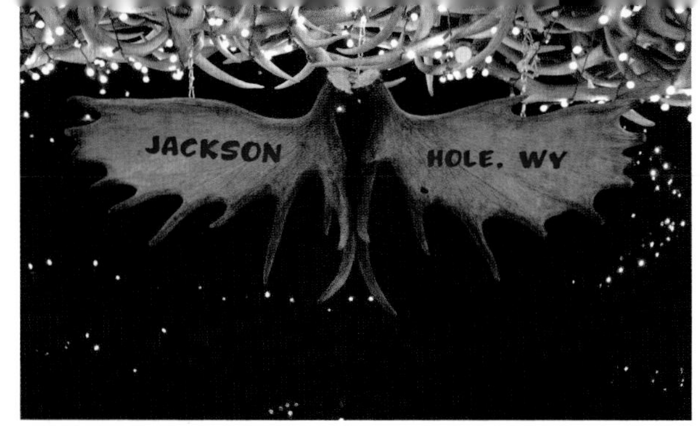

Antler Arch sign, 2012.

Jackson Town Square, circa 1950's. (Left to Right) George Lumley, John Wort, Walt King, Jack Francis, Harry Clissold, Slim Lawrence, Roy Jensen, Homer Richards, Cabot "CC" Cummins.

Antler Arch & Stagecoach, 2011.

Jackson Town Square

Originally part of the John and Maggie Simpson homestead, the Jackson Town Square was transformed by the local community from a treeless sagebrush depression to the tranquil park that one sees today. The Town of Jackson purchased the square in 1917 and the depression was slowly filled in as commercial buildings were built around the Town Square. In 1932, the park was leveled and landscaped with trees and grass as part of the nationwide celebration of George Washington's 200th birthday, and renamed George Washington Memorial Park. The beautification was made possible with contributions of local volunteers, the American Legion, and funds from the New Deal Civil Works Administration. The Rotary Club built the first of the Town Square's iconic elk antler arches on the southwest corner of the Town Square in 1953 (members integral to the construction of antler arches pictured here). The Town Square is the center of many community activities in Jackson and is listed on the National Register of Historic Places.

Jackson Hole Center for the Arts, 2011.

Jackson–Wilson High School, circa 1930's.

Jackson-Wilson High School

The Jackson–Wilson High School was built in 1929 to accommodate the increasing population in Jackson and surrounding communities. While today the old Jackson–Wilson High School is a memory, the site continues to serve the Jackson community in the form of the Jackson Hole Center for the Arts, which opened in 2004. The Center for the Arts consists of the 41,000 square foot Arts & Education Pavilion, as well as the Performing Arts Pavilion, which opened in 2007. The Arts & Education Pavilion is a multi-tenant facility housing, hosting, and partnering with seventeen local, state, and regional not-for-profit arts and higher education organizations.

The Wort Hotel

Charles J. Wort arrived in Jackson Hole in 1893. Staking claim just outside modern-day Jackson, Charles returned to his native Nebraska to marry Luella Perkins. The couple worked hard improving their claim and became successful cattle ranchers. Later in the 1930's, the Wort family operated what is now Signal Mountain Lodge in Grand Teton National Park guiding hunters and fishermen. It was through the sale of this facility, that the family financed construction of the Wort Hotel in 1941. The hotel was built by John and Jess Wort, fulfilling their father Charles Wort's dream of constructing a luxury hotel in Jackson. Erected on the four city lots Charles Wort paid $100 for in 1915, the Wort Hotel was encased in distinctive red stone quarried near Slide Lake in the Gros Ventre Mountains. The famous Silver Dollar Bar was added in 1950, and included a S-curved bar inlaid with 2,032 uncirculated 1921 Liberty Silver Dollars. The Wort has gone through many changes over the years, including a fire in 1980 that almost completely destroyed the hotel. The hotel was restored after the fire in 1981. "Meet me at the Wort" is a commonly heard phrase that has echoed through Jackson's history, and continues to be heard in present day.

While gambling in Wyoming has been illegal since 1901, gambling in remote Teton County remained common throughout the 1950's. The Wort had gambling in the Teton Room in the hotel's basement from its opening in 1941 until the late 1950's. Many pieces of original gambling equipment are still displayed in the hotel's public corridors.

The Wort Hotel, circa late 1940's.

Gambling in Jackson, circa late 1940's.

The Wort Hotel, 2011.

Silver Dollar Bar, 2011.

Interior, the Wort Hotel lobby, 2011.

Antler Motel, 2005.

The Virginian Lodge, 2009.

The Motel Era

The word motel, a combination of motor and hotel or motorists' hotel, referred originally to a type of hotel consisting of a single building of connected rooms whose doors faced a parking lot or common area. Some motels consisted of a series of small cabins with common parking. As the United States highway system began to develop in the 1920s, long distance road journeys became more common and the need for inexpensive, easily accessible overnight accommodation close to main automobile routes led to the growth of the motel concept, and Jackson was no exception. Conveniently located on U.S. Highway 89, motor tourism through Jackson boomed during the 1930's and continued well into the 1950's. Today, the automobile remains the main mode of transportation for tourists visiting Jackson, Grand Teton National Park, and Yellowstone National Park.

Left: Kudar Motel sign, 2007. Above: Kudar Motel sign, 2011.

Kudar Motel

For many tourists visiting Jackson time and time again, their first trips were spent at the Kudar Motel. Many adults have nostalgic memories of playing as kids under the big cottonwood trees in the common area. Perhaps a favorite memory is the first night spent in a rustic cabin. Built in 1938, the Kudar Motel has been owned and operated by the Kudar family for two generations. Still in business today and creating new memories, the Kudar is a glimpse of a bygone era.

Mickey Hicks on Billy the Kid, Jackson Hole Rodeo, circa 1940's.

Frontier Days, Frontier Park, circa 1950's.

Jackson Hole Rodeo, 2011.

Frontier Days: 100 years of the Jackson Hole Rodeo

Frontier Days began in 1912 as Jackson Hole's first community celebration. Local sponsors built a grandstand on land southwest of town that later became known as "Frontier Park". The Jackson Hole Rodeo is still primarily a local affair with most cowboys coming from area ranches and second and third generation Teton County families. The Jackson Hole Rodeo runs on weekends from Memorial Day through Labor Day, entertaining locals and tourists alike.

Dude Ranching in Jackson Hole

Seeking a way to make cattle ranching financially profitable in the harsh and marginal environment of Jackson Hole, many ranchers began hosting tourists or "dudes" at their ranches during the summer months. Dude ranching was a natural outgrowth of the hunting and fishing guide business that many cattle ranchers had been conducting since the early 1900's. With abundant scenery and plentiful wildlife, Jackson Hole became a prime destination for individuals seeking to "rough it" out West. It can also not be underestimated the influence dude ranching had on pioneering the tourism industry in the western United States in general, and specifically in Jackson Hole. The first dude ranch in Jackson Hole was the JY Ranch in 1908, followed closely by the Bar BC in 1912 and the White Grass Ranch in 1919. Others soon followed including the Half Moon Ranch, the STS, the Danny Ranch, the Trail Ranch, the Red Rock, the Castle Rock, the Circle H, the Triangle X, and the Double Diamond among others.

Union Pacific Railroad brochure, circa 1930's.

Dude Ranches Out West

DAWN flaming over the hills in a sighing, beckoning wilderness of spruce and pine—the refreshing babble of a tumbling mountain brook—neighing horses—ravishing aroma of bubbling coffee and crisping bacon—would you like to wake up and discover all this?

Far from the crowded city, where pavements give place to wooded trails, where life on the open prairies is varied by pack trips to the haunts of mountain trout, a *real* vacation awaits you.

The "Dude Ranches" of the West make you free of the great outdoors. The "wranglers" who operate them extend a hospitable welcome to the "dude" and teach him the ways of the West, its wisdom and its beauty.

This booklet is a round-up of facts about "Dude Ranches" and resorts reached via the Union Pacific. Any Union Pacific representative listed on page 47 will gladly help you plan your vacation. Put foot to stirrup, reader, and we'll go out West!

Union Pacific Railroad brochure, circa 1930's.

The Jackson Hole Gang

Author's note: Conducting research for a historical photography project can be time consuming. Many hours are spent sifting through photographs. Computer and online databases have made the task easier, but only by a matter of degrees. Occasionally you run across a photograph that captures the essence of a subject or an idea. The photograph seen here that I personally refer to as "The Jackson Hole Gang," is just such an image. The beaming smiles on the women's faces, and the tired yet satisfied posture of each individual, speaks to the concept of dude ranching as a worthy recreational activity. It also explains in one glimpse, why dude ranches were so popular for their time.

Group of "Girl Dudes," Turpin Meadows Dude Ranch, circa 1932.

White Grass Ranch

The White Grass Ranch was established as a cattle ranch in 1913 by Harold Hammond and George Tucker Bispham. The White Grass was converted to a dude ranch in 1919, and along with the JY and Bar BC, became one of the first dude ranches in Jackson Hole. Located at the base of the Teton Range near the mouth of Stewart Draw, the White Grass Ranch consisted of ten guest cabins, a lodge, a dining hall, and a laundry building. Ownership of the White Grass eventually passed to Hammond's son-in-law Frank Galey who continued the operation until his death in 1985, making it one of the longest-lived active dude ranches in Jackson Hole. Today, the White Grass Ranch is being rehabilitated as a training facility and cultural resource center for the Western Center for Historic Preservation.

Above: White Grass Ranch Lodge, circa 1940's. Below: interior, White Grass Ranch, circa 1940's.

Above: White Grass Ranch Lodge, 2011. Below: interior, White Grass Ranch Lodge, 2011

Vintage White Grass Ranch poster, circa 1950's.

The Western Center for Historic Preservation

The Western Center for Historic Preservation was jointly developed by the National Park Service and the National Trust for Historic Preservation, and is an education and resource center dedicated to the preservation and maintenance of cultural resources in our western national parks. The White Grass Ranch rehabilitation project is scheduled to be completed in 2016.

Bar BC Ranch

The Bar BC Ranch was established by Struthers Burt and Dr. Horace Carncross in 1912. Burt was a popular eastern writer and published articles and novels that attracted fellow writers to his dude ranch. With a constant stream of literary figures visiting the Bar BC, the ranch began to gain a reputation as a lively and entertaining place to stay and "rough it." During its heyday, the Bar BC consisted of over 100 buildings including the main lodge, dance hall, dude cabins, horse barn, corrals, and two swimming pools fed by water diverted from the nearby Snake River. Today, only a fraction of the 100 structures remain. However, as one strolls through the ruins of the Bar BC, one can almost hear the laughter of dudes dancing into the late hours of the night. The Bar BC Ranch is now part of Grand Teton National Park, who in cooperation with the Western Center for Historic Preservation, plan on preserving what remains of the Bar BC as an interpretive site.

Above: Bar BC Ranch, circa 1940's. Below: Bar BC Ranch, 2011

Derelict automobile, Bar BC Ranch, 2011.

Interior, Main Lodge, Bar BC Ranch, 2011.

Chimney, Main Lodge, Bar BC Ranch, 2011.

Triangle X Ranch

John S. and Maytie Turner established the Triangle X Ranch in 1927 on the former Bill Jump homestead. In a few short years the Triangle X totaled 320 acres and consisted of a large headquarters building and six dude cabins. John and Maytie Turner sold the Triangle X Ranch to the Snake River Land Company in 1929, with the company leasing the property back to the Turners to operate as a dude ranch. The Triangle X was eventually incorporated into the new Grand Teton National Park, and in 1953, John C. Turner secured a concession permit to operate the dude ranch his father started. Over the years, successive generations of the Turner family have operated the Triangle X, which is the longest operating dude ranch in Jackson Hole. Today, the Triangle X Ranch has grown to include a main lodge, 21 guest cabins, a gift shop, and several other buildings associated with the Triangle X's horseback rides, float trips, and fishing trips.

Above: Dudes at the Triangle X Ranch, date unknown. Below: Saddles Triangle X Ranch, 2011.

Triangle X barn, 2011.

Interior, Main Lodge, Triangle X Ranch, 2011.

Triangle X sign, 2009.

Elbo Ranch Rodeo grounds, circa 1920's.

Elbo Ranch

The Elbo Ranch was created after James Manges sold his homestead in 1926 to Chester Goss. Assembling a total of 423 acres through the purchase of the neighboring Frank and Albert Bessette ranches, Goss was able to expand the Elbo's guest accommodations, as well as build a rodeo ground, racetrack, and grandstand. Like many other landowners, Goss sold out to the Snake River Land Company in 1929 and the property eventually passed into the hands of the National Park Service as part of an expanded Grand Teton National Park. Today, nothing remains from the Elbo Ranch, save the original Manges Cabin.

Former Elbo Ranch Rodeo grounds site, 2011.

Danny Ranch

In 1922, Tony Grace established the Danny Ranch on a 160-acre homestead east of String Lake. The ranch originally consisted of a three-room lodge, two guest cabins, and a barn. By 1927, the Danny Ranch featured four guest cabins, but was still one of the smallest dude ranches in Jackson Hole. Grace sold the Danny Ranch to the Snake River Land Company in 1930. The property was renovated and renamed the Jenny Lake Ranch in the late 1930's, and has been a tourist destination since that time. Today, Tony Grace's original residence forms a portion of the Jenny Lake Lodge.

Above: Jenny Lake Lodge cabins, 2011. Below: Danny Ranch, circa 1930's.

Above: Jenny Lake Lodge, 2011. Below: interior, Jenny Lake Lodge, 2011.

Jenny Lake Lodge

The Jenny Lake Lodge has evolved considerably from its humble beginnings in the 1920's. What was once one of the smallest and most rustic dude ranches in the valley, now features elegantly appointed cabins, as well as gourmet breakfasts and five-course dinners in the Jenny Lake Lodge dining room. However, horseback rides are still a standard activity for most guests. The Jenny Lake Lodge is operated by the Grand Teton Lodge Company.

4 Lazy F Ranch lodge, circa 1950's.

4 Lazy F Ranch

The 4 Lazy F Ranch was built originally as the Sun Star Ranch by Bryant Mears in 1915, and consisted of two cabins, a barn, and a corral. William Frew purchased the ranch in 1927 after spending time at the Bar BC Ranch in 1924. Frew renamed the ranch the 4 Lazy F Ranch for the "Four Lazy Frews" and immediately began improving the ranch with a main lodge and several additional guest cabins. While styled after a traditional dude ranch, the Frew's primarily used the 4 Lazy F as a private retreat, although they did accept paying guests at the family's invitation. Emily Frew Oliver sold the 4 Lazy F Ranch to the National Park Service in 1967, retaining a life estate. Due to Emily Frew Oliver's declining health, the Frew family conveyed the 4 Lazy F to the National Park Service in 2006. Upon transferring the property, the Frew family expressed hope that the 4 Lazy F would remain available to the public and preserved in order to educate people about the history of dude ranches and the vital role they played in shaping the history of Jackson Hole.

Above: 4 Lazy F Ranch barn, 2011. Below: 4 Lazy F Ranch cabin, 2011.

Grand Teton National Park

Grand Teton National Park was established in 1929, protecting the Teton Range and six lakes located at the base of the range. However, the valley of Jackson Hole remained primarily in private ownership and open to development. John D. Rockefeller Jr. and his wife visited Jackson Hole in the late 1920's and were both awed by the beauty of the Teton Range, and disturbed by the rampant commercial development occurring around such pristine areas as Jenny Lake. In an effort to protect the valley and its scenic qualities, Rockefeller latched onto a plan first broached in a historic meeting at Maude Noble's cabin on July 26, 1923. At the meeting, Yellowstone National Park Superintendent Horace Albright discussed with a small group of locals, the idea of finding funds for the purchase of private lands in Jackson Hole to donate to a future expanded Grand Teton National Park. In 1927, Rockefeller formed the Snake River Land Company to facilitate the purchase of over 32,000 acres of private lands in the valley. In 1943, President Franklin Delano Roosevelt created the Jackson Hole National Monument, which preserved much of the valley under control of the federal government. An expanded Grand Teton National Park, which merged the original park with the Jackson Hole National Monument, came to fruition in 1950 after over 20 years of controversy. At the end of 1949, John D. Rockefeller Jr. gifted 32,177 acres to the United States and its citizens, completing the mission of the historic meeting in Maude Noble's cabin over a quarter-century prior.

Entrance, Grand Teton National Park, 2012.

Horace Albright, Grand Teton National Park dedication, 1929.

Above: Jenny Lake Junction, circa 1930's. Below: North Jenny Lake Junction, 2011.

Jenny Lake Junction

After the establishment of Grand Teton National Park in 1929, automobile tourism became a significant mode of seeing the park for many individuals. This development created a new host of issues for a fledgling park administration to deal with including dust, road maintenance, noise, and traffic.

Above: former Moran town site & Jackson Lake Dam, 2011. Below: Moran & Jackson Lake Dam, circa 1920's.

Moran & Jackson Lake Dam

The town of Moran was situated at the outlet of Jackson Lake on the northern bank of the Snake River. Established in the early 1900's, Moran was the site of Ben Sheffield's Teton Lodge Resort, as well as a toll bridge that was the main transportation corridor for travelers heading north to Yellowstone. The town boasted a hotel, saloon, livery stable, general store, and post office. Moran boomed during the construction of the Jackson Lake Dam from 1910 to 1916. The Sheffield's sold their holdings to the Snake River Land Company in 1929. The operations were phased out and buildings removed by the National Park Service in the 1950's. Today, the former town site has largely been reclaimed by nature.

Harrison Crandall Studio, circa 1928.

Interior, Jenny Lake Visitor Center, 2011.

Jenny Lake Visitor Center, 2011.

Harrison Crandall Studio

Harrison Crandall homesteaded with his wife Hildegarde in 1924 near String Lake. Determined to make a living as a photographer, Crandall photographed Jackson Hole's abundant natural beauty as well as its unique culture of ranchers, dudes, and tourists. In 1926, Crandall built a log studio to sell his photographs. When the Snake River Land Company offered to purchase their property in 1929, the Crandalls took the offer. Harrison Crandall won a concession permit soon thereafter, and moved his studio to its present site at Jenny Lake. Harrison Crandall retired in 1959 leaving a photographic legacy that gives testament to Jackson Hole's colorful history. The former Crandall Studio is now the Jenny Lake Visitor Center.

The Chapel of the Transfiguration, circa 1930's.

The Chapel of the Transfiguration

The Chapel of the Transfiguration is located in Moose, just west of Menor's Ferry. The Episcopal chapel was built in 1925 to serve the many dude ranches that had been established in the immediate area. Maude Noble donated the land for the chapel. Local ranchers provided construction materials and labor, while Mr. C.B. Voorhis contributed the majority of the funding. The Chapel of the Transfiguration has become a favorite wedding destination with untold numbers of couples reciting wedding vows in the shadow of the Teton Range.

Interior, The Chapel of the Transfiguration, 2011.

Stained glass window, 2011.

The Chapel of the Transfiguration, 2003.

Above: Overlook, Jenny Lake, 2011. Right: Overlook, Jenny Lake, circa 1930's.

Jenny Lake

Jenny Lake was named for "Beaver Dick" Leigh's Shoshone wife Jenny. The Hayden Expedition of 1872 named Leigh and Jenny lakes for the Leigh's invaluable guiding assistance, breaking from the tradition of naming landmarks after expedition team members. Leigh's wife Jenny and their six children died of smallpox in 1876. Jenny Lake became the focal point of commercial development during the 1920's that ultimately led to the preservation of the Jackson Hole valley in an expanded Grand Teton National Park in 1950. Today, Jenny Lake is one of the busiest tourist centers in Grand Teton National Park supporting a variety of activities including hiking, biking, boating, fishing, climbing, and camping.

Moose Store & Post Office, circa 1940's.

Dornans Chuckwagon, circa 1950's

Moose — Dornans

Menor's Ferry became known as Moose, when in 1929 the Moose Post Office was relocated to the local schoolhouse. The steel truss bridge built in 1927 that rendered the Menor's Ferry obsolete brought with it increasing automobile traffic. To capitalize on the traffic, many tourist related businesses sprung up around Moose, including a store and gas station that housed the Moose Post Office. On the east side of the Snake River, Evelyn Dornan and her son Jack developed tourist facilities to meet demand as well. Dornans became well known for their Dornans Chuckwagon, which has been feeding hungry locals and visitors every summer since 1948. Other facilities present today at Dornans are guest cabins, restaurants, wine store, gift shop, and adventure sports rentals.

Dornans Chuckwagon, 2011.

Signal Mountain Lodge, circa 1968.

Signal Mountain Lodge, 2011.

Signal Mountain Lodge

Located on the eastern shore of Jackson Lake, Signal Mountain Lodge started as a fishing camp in the 1920's. Charles Wort purchased the camp in 1931 and expanded the facility to include a lodge, gas station, and several visitor cabins. The Wort family sold the lodge in 1941 to the Harris family in order to finance construction of the Wort Hotel in Jackson. The Harris family owned and operated Signal Mountain Lodge until the 1980's, and was responsible for the development of the majority of Signal Mountain's facilities including the lake front cabins, restaurant and gift shop building, convenience store, and main lodge. Today, Signal Mountain Lodge is owned and operated by Rex Maughan under a National Park Service concession permit.

Jackson Lake Lodge (original Amoretti Inn), circa 1940's.

Above: construction, Jackson Lake Lodge, 1955. Below: Jackson Lake Lodge, 2011.

Jackson Lake Lodge

The Jackson Lake Lodge is located on a bluff above Willow Flats, with a sublime view of Jackson Lake and the Teton Range. Recognizing a need for modern lodging in the newly expanded Grand Teton National Park, John D. Rockefeller, Jr. set about building a new lodge on the site originally occupied by Eugene Amoretti's Amoretti Inn from 1924 to 1953. Construction of the Jackson Lake Lodge commenced in 1955. Designed by Gilbert Stanley Underwood, the architecture of the Jackson Lake Lodge represented a break with the traditional rustic style of architecture typically used in the National Park Service. The Jackson Lake Lodge was designated a National Historic Landmark in 2003.

Interior, Jackson Lake Lodge, 2011.

Jackson Lake Lodge, 1955.

Jackson Lake Lodge, 2011.

Left: Snow King Resort, 2012. Above: Snow King Resort, circa 1950's.

Skiing in Jackson Hole: A Brief History

In the 1930's, lifts and rope tows were built in Moose Creek, north of Victor, Idaho, as well as Signal Mountain, Two Ocean Mountain, and Leek's Canyon. Jackson's first ski race was held on Snow King in 1937 with skiers racing down a Forest Service hiking trail that was cut by the Civilian Conservation Corps. In 1939, Snow King opened for business with the Old Man Flat rope tow. Wyoming's first chair lift came to Snow King in 1946. Snow King quickly became the place where all the kids in Jackson Hole learned to ski. Later in 1965, Jackson Hole Mountain Resort opened on Rendezvous Mountain, complete with a modern aerial tram. Today, Snow King Resort is still the "locals" mountain where someone can blow off a couple hours of work and get in a few turns. However, like many small recreational ski hills, Snow King is struggling financially. Meanwhile, Jackson Hole Mountain Resort has grown into a destination resort and includes 2,500 acres of terrain, ten chairlifts, one gondola, and a new aerial tram.

Jackson Hole Mountain Resort, circa late 1960's.

Jackson Hole Mountain Resort, 2011.

Teton Village, 2012.

Cinema in Jackson Hole

Above: Alan Ladd and Jean Arthur from "Shane", 1953. Below: Luther Taylor Homestead, 2011.

The Teton Range west of Jackson Hole provides arguably one of the most beautiful and scenic backdrops in the world. Photographers from William Henry Jackson to Ansel Adams have captured the grandeur of the Tetons. Hollywood movies also have utilized the dramatic scenery of Jackson Hole, including the iconic 1953 western *Shane* starring Alan Ladd and Jean Arthur. The movie utilized such set locations as Antelope Flats, Schwabacher's Landing, Mormon Row, and the Luther Taylor Homestead. Other movies filmed in Jackson Hole include *The Big Trail, Bad Bascomb, Spencer's Mountain, Wyoming,* and *The Big Sky.*

Sundance Inn demolition, 2011.

Postcard, the Flame Motel, circa 1950's.

Sundance Inn demolition, 2011.

Afterword – The Sundance Inn

Originally built as the Flame Motel in the early 1950's, the Sundance Inn was demolished in the fall of 2011. Due to its visibility along the Highway 89 entry corridor, the Sundance represents a significant loss to the vintage character of Jackson Hole. The description on the back of the Flame Motel postcard pictured here, speaks of the changes that have taken place in the last six decades. The postcard describes the motel in part as a "quiet fireproof resting place", and featuring such modern comforts as "baseboard hot water heat, wall to wall carpets, tile baths and tangy western décor." Today, the former motel site has been converted into a parking lot.

Photography Credits & Notes

Photograph Credits:
Front Cover: Rick Pieros
Back Cover: Back Cover: Collection of the Jackson Hole Historical Society and Museum, 1958.0226.001 (top), and Rick Pieros (bottom)

Collection of the Jackson Hole Society and Museum:
1991.3561.001 Trapper "Beaver Dick" Leigh 8, 1958.0491.01 Menor's Ferry (bottom) 10, 2004.0102.667 Manges Cabin (middle) 12, 1992.4156.001 Norman Smith Homestead (top) 13, 1958.0953.001 Edith Drake Sargent 14, hs.4269.10 John Moulton homestead 16, 1958.2352.0001 Miller House (top left) 18, 1991.3568.001 Miller House (bottom) 19, p96.0009 Wilson Post Office (top) 20, 1958.2402.001 Episcopal Church (top right) 21, 1958.0223.001 Teton Pass (top) 22, 1991.4046.001 Teton Pass (top) 23, 1958.0225.001 Jackson 24, 1958.4257.001 Clubhouse Building 26, 1958.0386.001 Deloney's (top right) 28, 1958.0231.001 Hotel Jackson (bottom) 29, 1958.1054.001 St. John's (top) 30 & 31, 1991.3973.001 Coe Cabin (top) 32, 1958.3292.001 Crabtree Hotel (top) 33, 1958.2227.001 Jackson State Bank (top left) 34, 1992.4201.001 Jackson State Bank (top right) 34, 1992.4233.001 American Legion Hall (top) 35, 1958.0387.001 Spicer Garage 36, 1958.1265.0001 Simpson Hardware (right) 38, 1958.0237.0001 Miller House (bottom) 39, 1958.2467.001 Van Vleck House (left) 40, 1958.0090.001 Jackson Town Council (top) 41, 2003.0050.009 Jackson Drug 42, 1958.1201.001 Mercill's (top) 44,1991.3776.0031 Silver Spur Café (top left) 45, 1958.0560.001 Cowboy Bar 46, 1991.3942.001 Teton Theater (right) 48, 1958.3382.001 Rotary Club – Antler Arch (bottom left) 50, 2008.0016.001 Jackson–Wilson High School (bottom) 51, 2004.0004.032 The Wort Hotel (top) 1958.2349.001 Gambling in Jackson (bottom) 52, 1958.1807.001 Mickey Hicks (top) 1958.1478.001 Frontier Days (bottom) 56, Union Pacific Brochure (right/left) 58, 2008.0044.013 White Grass Ranch Lodge (top) 1958.2533.001 Interior, White Grass Ranch (bottom) 60, 1996.0005.001 Bar BC Ranch (top) 62, 2005.0016.028 Triangle X Ranch (top) 64, 1958.2223.001 Elbo Ranch 66, 2003.0007.002 Danny Ranch (bottom) 68, 1958.2031.01 4 Lazy F Ranch 70, 1993.4922.0001 Jenny Lake Junction (top) 73, 1958.2769.001 Jackson Lake Dam (bottom) 74, 1992.4225.001 Harrison Crandall Studio (top left) 75, 1958.2404.001 The Chapel of the Transfiguration 76, bc.0203 Jenny Lake 79, 1993.4941.001 Moose Store (top left) 80, 1958.1032.001 Jackson Lake Lodge (top left) 2003.0074.006 Jackson Lake Lodge (top right) 82, 2003.0074.057 Jackson Lake Lodge (bottom left) 83, 1999.0031.001 Snow King Resort (right) 84, 1998.0065.0001 Jackson Hole Mountain Resort (top) 85, 1958.2771.002 Shane (top) 86

American Heritage Center, University of Wyoming:
Jackson Hole Rodeo Grounds-Stephen Leek Collection, Box 100 pgs. 4 & 5, Hayden Expedition – Fritoif Fryxell Collection 6, Dude Girls – Karl C. Allen Collection 59, Dornans Chuckwagon – Jackson Hole, Chuckwagon Photograph File (top right) 80

National Archives and Records Administration:
National Archives and Records Administration: Photograph No. 517661; Teton Range and Jackson Lake, Wyoming, 1872, Department of the Interior, General Land Office, U.S. Geographic Survey of the Territories, (1874 –1879); National Archives and Records Administration, Still Pictures Records Section, National Archives at College Park, MD (top left) 7

National Park Service:
Bill Menor (top left) 10, Menor's Ferry (top) 10, Grand Teton National Park Dedication (bottom) 72

Signal Mountain Lodge:
Signal Mountain Lodge (top) 81

Public Domain:
William Henry Jackson (top right) 7, The Flame Motel (top right) 87

Book design by Riverbed Design, riverbeddesign.com

Photography Notes ~ Rick Pieros:
The photographic work by Rick Pieros represented in *Jackson Hole 1878 to 2012: Historical Photographs Past to Present* was photographed using traditional film, as well as digital capture methods. Rick Pieros uses a variety of camera mediums including 35mm, DSLR, and medium format cameras.

Ivy Rasmussen (author's grandmother), Jenny Lake, 1978.